nature
INSPIRED
JOURNAL

4-weeks of Journaling Pages and
Prompts for Your Reflective Practice

Companion to the Nature-inspired Deck Series
Fauna Inspiration · Flora Healing · Fantastic Being

Rebecca Lefebvre BSW, BSN, RN

AVECLAVIE.COM

About the
AUTHOR

Rebecca is trained as a social worker and registered nurse. In 2014, after witnessing years of pain and suffering, she founded Avec La Vie. Since then she has created numerous decks and written multiple books to normalize mental wellness, promote whole-health, and inspire conscious, purposeful living.

Now, a full-time author and artist, Rebecca lives in Colorado with her family, an ever-expanding perennial garden as well as five chickens, three dogs, a few koi fish, and one very fickle cat.

She hopes her creations instill thoughtfulness and tranquility–juxtaposing the harsh angles of our world with welcomed transcendence.

AVECLAVIE.COM

Nature-inspired journal:
4-weeks of journaling pages and prompts for your reflective practice

An Imprint of Avec La Vie, LLC
PO Box 627
Broomfield, CO 80020

ISBN 978-0-9972560-9-3

Printed in America

aveclavie.com

Cover photo: Daria Shevtsova (pexels.com)
Book design: Rebecca Lefebvre
Interior image and illustration credits: Rebecca Lefebvre, Phoebe Hunt, istock, and pexels.com

DISCLAIMER: THE MATERIAL PRESENTED IN THIS PUBLICATION IS NOT AN ATTEMPT TO PRACTICE MEDICINE OR GIVE SPECIFIC MEDICAL ADVICE, INCLUDING, WITHOUT LIMITATION, ADVICE CONCERNING THE TOPIC OF MENTAL HEALTH. The information contained in this book is for the sole purpose of being informative and is not to be considered complete, and does not cover all issues related to mental health. Moreover, this information should not replace consultation with your doctor or other qualified mental health providers and/or specialists. If you believe you or another individual is suffering a mental health crisis or other medical emergency, contact your doctor immediately–or seek medical attention immediately in an emergency room or call 911.

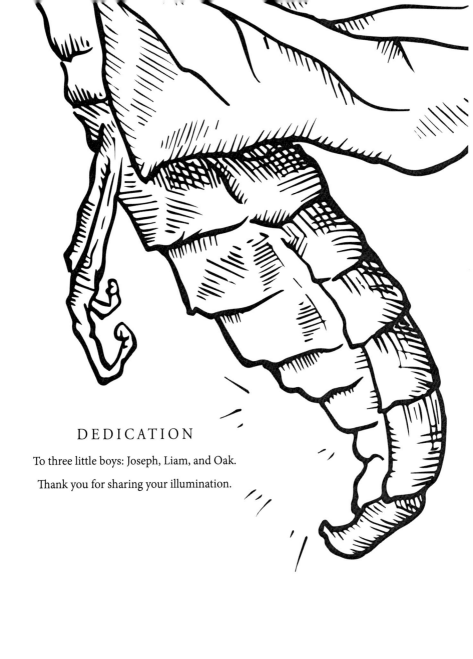

DEDICATION

To three little boys: Joseph, Liam, and Oak.

Thank you for sharing your illumination.

ACKNOWLEDGMENTS

To you my friend—you are a bright light, let yourself shine!

CONTENTS

The Art of Journaling

THE ART OF JOURNALING

I remember vividly the very first diary I had as a child. It was the size of my hand. After scratching my secrets onto its pages, I would lock it with a shiny gold key and hide it under my bed. In a house full of boys, everything about that ritual was special to me.

Sadly, I lost my diary during one of our many moves. Thinking back, I bet I placed it on a shelf or one of my brothers hid it from me. Either way, whoever found it probably held hope my scribble would read like a Anne Frank diary. Lucky for me my formative years were less intense than Anne's. However, I did experience my fair share of fear, isolation, and assault. I was the youngest child of an alcoholic father who was prone to bouts of verbal and physical abuse. Also, when I was about ten years old, I was molested by a teenage boy who lived next door. With few places to share how I was feeling, I religiously cataloged my experiences in that diary. Surely, my entries would have revealed a confused little girl trying to make sense of the world around her.

On a positive note, writing down what was happening to me (and around me) taught me how to express myself. With reflection and contemplation, I could look at my life from different perspectives. Those early notations helped me realize: I was not my father. I was an independent person with distinct values and beliefs. I could choose to be different. I didn't have to be like him or be with anyone who treated me like our neighbor. In fact, I remember making a promise to myself in that diary that read something like this: "I won't be like my dad or _ever_ marry someone who is mean to me or the people I love."

Upon reflection, it is safe to say my inner inquiry revealed a lot about what I wanted for myself and who I wanted to be when I grew up. Nevertheless, life pushed me forward and my young proclamations were put to the test. For example, even though I penned my sentiments like I was writing the ten commandments, middle school and high school made sticking to them hard. Not all of my boyfriends were kind to me (nor were my girlfriends for that matter) and I didn't learn how to be true to myself or choose friends wisely until much later. It wasn't until the end of my freshman year in college I decided to take control of my life.

After a long, mediocre relationship, I finally understood that my intentions weren't going to materialize until I put in the effort; which would require me to make some tough choices to achieve my goals. When I returned home that summer, I was scared and overwhelmed. I sat in my room for a few days and cried. After a lot of excuses and a fair amount of deflecting, I began a new journal. At the top of the first page I wrote: "That will never happen again–exclamation point, exclamation point, exclamation point." (Coincidence or conviction, I will never know but within a month I met the man who would later become my husband. Since then, we have been together for nearly thirty years.)

That being said, the past three decades haven't always been easy. Every day I have to be mindful of my thoughts, emotions, and choices. It is easy for them to lead me astray, especially when I walk into my days robotic or careless.

Additionally, life has taught me: Committing to personal growth requires finding your truth, embracing it, *and* sharing it with the people in your life. As scary as being imperfect and authentic is, those particular stepping-stones are necessary for healing and change.

To that end, I believe writing is an art that is best expressed by the heart. As a mindfulness tool, I have found it to be a reliable way to further one's wellness journey. Used consistently, reflective journaling can help you cultivate self-trust, strengthen your intuition, and reveal who you are and how you want to live. For example, the more you know about yourself the easier it becomes to say "no" to what you don't want and "yes" to what you do, such as personal boundaries to protect your values and experiences balanced by comfort and joy.

In closing, as you read through these pages and practice reflecting, I hope this journal encourages you to take a few moments to slow down, be honest with yourself, and manifest your soul's intentions–consciously and purposefully. Because, even though life can be bullish, you can choose how to experience each day.

With love,
Rebecca Lefebvre

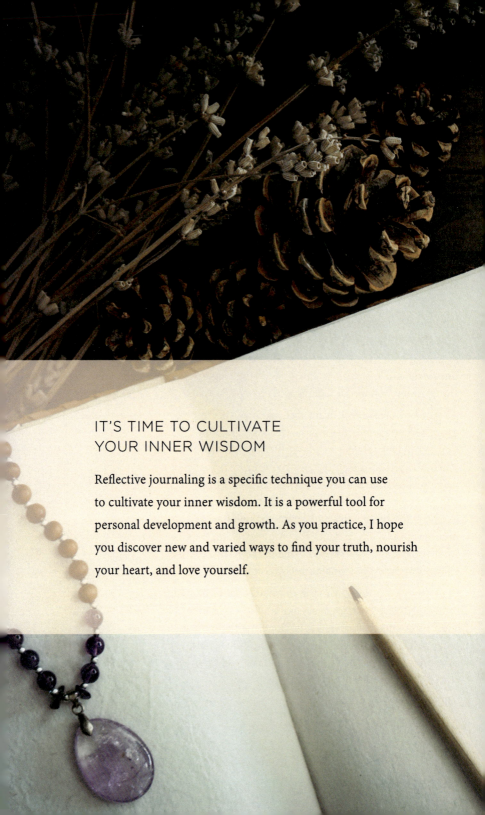

IT'S TIME TO CULTIVATE
YOUR INNER WISDOM

Reflective journaling is a specific technique you can use
to cultivate your inner wisdom. It is a powerful tool for
personal development and growth. As you practice, I hope
you discover new and varied ways to find your truth, nourish
your heart, and love yourself.

THE JOURNAL

---

*Sacred time to get
curious & express yourself*

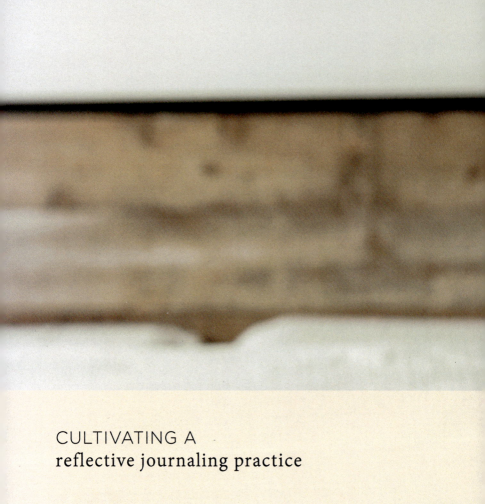

CULTIVATING A
reflective journaling practice

JOURNAL FORMAT

This reflective journal has been created to introduce you to a particular form of journaling I discovered while I was writing my three nature-inspired decks. I refer to this practice as contemplative writing. It is a mindfulness and self-expression method that includes four stepping-stones to help you define who you are and how you want to live.

* * *

For simplicity, I have divided the journal into four sections:

1. **CULTIVATING A REFLECTIVE JOURNALING PRACTICE**

   In this opening section I provide a description of reflective journaling and why it should be an integral component of your wellness practice. Additionally, I have included instructions on how to use the journaling pages, an emotion wheel to help you identify and become familiar with your feelings, and an explanation of the elements on the back of each card.

2. **JOURNALING PAGES**

   This section is the heart of the journal. It includes twenty-eight journaling pages, designed to be used with any of the nature-inspired decks, as well as four Planned Reflection pages. Each journaling page has a "prewrite" and "reflection" exercise as well as a writing prompt on the corresponding open page. Every seven days use the Planned Reflections pages to explore your entries and gain insight into yourself.

3. **JOURNAL SUMMARY**

   Once you are have completed the twenty-eight journaling pages, use the journal summary activities to consolidate what you have learned about yourself and identify your soul's intentions. Combined, these two elements form the foundation for the next step of the reflective journaling process titled Action Planning.

4. **ACTION PLANNING**

   This section includes four goal setting activities (complete with micro-steps and date planning) to help you plan your journey and get you where you want to go.

CULTIVATING A REFLECTIVE JOURNALING PRACTICE

WHAT IS REFLECTIVE JOURNALING?

If you have ever searched for a way to learn about yourself, express your emotions, or decipher the meaning of life you have probably heard of journaling. It is one of the most widely-used forms of self-reflection and is recommended by mental health professionals around the world.

Typically, the journaling process incorporates an unstructured, free-writing method to capture your daily experiences. Recent developments, by mindfulness practitioners and people interested in increasing their productivity, have introduced dots, lines, and glyphs you can use to help organize your "to do" lists.

As powerful and effective as these self-help methods are, they aren't specifically designed to identify the barriers, patterns, and relationships that limit you from achieving healthier, holistic outcomes. Nor are they constructed to align your day-to-day activities with your life intentions.

This is where reflective journaling shines. With a few additional elements and a consistent writing process, reflective journaling becomes a contemplative writing exercise for intentional living. For example, the four stepping-stones introduced in this journal invite you to cultivate your inner wisdom for personal and professional development.

By using the Journaling Pages to express yourself, you will be able to explore archetypal concepts such as self-love, personal responsibility, and self-trust; which are important elements of self-actualization.

Then, every seven days you will complete a Planned Reflection. Each of these "look backs" will help you discover patterns and opportunities to heal old wounds and consider ways to move forward and grow.

Once you have completed the journaling pages, the Journal Summary and Action Planning activities can help you isolate your specific life intentions and create action steps to turn your goals into reality.

THE FOUR STEPPING-STONES

While helping people navigate complex situations, I identified three elements that individuals, families, and teams consistently used to achieve their goals. These included: awareness, reflection, and action. Collectively, I refer to these three concepts as the Circle of Change.

For example, the first thing any of us needs to do to address our *dis*ease or illness is to identify what is making us sick. That might sound obvious but *knowing* the root cause (i.e., the primary reason or reasons for our discomfort) is actually harder than you might think. We are complex

CIRCLE OF CHANGE

Awareness . Reflection . Action

entities. Many of our problems are a result of a series of events and/or a host of factors. Consequently, it can take a while to discover the principle problems we need to address to improve our lives.

The second stage of change requires *reflection*. Again, this can be hard. Acknowledging and labeling the causes we have identified as "problematic" can create internal and external conflict. It is difficult to admit to and analyze our unhealthy choices and patterns or imbalanced relationships. This is why I believe self-reflection and personal responsibility benefit greatly from objectivity, logic, and self-love.

Last but not least, the Circle of Change requires *action*. For many of us, this is the greatest challenge of all. Manifesting change requires self-trust, creativity, and persistence. These can be hard to embody and easily negated by self-limiting beliefs and societal pressures.

That being said, if we really want to achieve wellness, we have to experience the Circle of Change. This is why I have woven these concepts into the four stepping-stones of the reflective journaling process described below.

Step One: Prompted Self-Inquiry*

As noted above, this stepping-stone is first and foremost about awareness. Of all the activities in this methodology, it is by far the easiest skill to practice. Simply pull a card from one of the three nature-inspired decks, read the message, and think about it. The goal is to gain greater knowledge of who you are, how you want to be, and how other people, traditions, and norms can affect the outcome of your efforts.

Unique to this step, prompted self-inquiry **does not** require writing. If you only have a few moments to be present for yourself, this stepping-stone offers the simplest, most flexible way for you to think about life and consider its meaning. For example, I like to pull a card, read it, and then go for a walk or tend to my garden. Alone time (a.k.a., ponder time) helps me process the content of the card and consider what it really means to me.

*Prompted self-inquiry does not need to be limited to the nature-inspired decks. Anything that begs for consideration is a potential prompt for self-reflection (e.g., an encounter with an animal, a conversation with a friend, a conflict at work, or a trip to the grocery store) to better understand yourself and the world around you.

WHAT IS REFLECTIVE JOURNALING?

Reflective journaling is a method of inner inquiry and expression that encourages you to examine your thoughts, feelings, and ideas. By being aware of these things, you can identify the tools, skills, or knowledge you need to confront the challenges you face. Self-reflection can also help you determine if you and/or your wellness journey might benefit from the support of others such as a coach, mentor, therapist, and other wellness professional. These individuals are equipped with a myriad of reliable ways to help you work through complex situations and relationships and set realistic goals to achieve your intentions and life goals.

THE FOUR STEPPING-STONES OF REFLECTIVE JOURNALING

1. **Prompted Self-inquiry**
   GOAL: Become aware

2. **Contemplative Writing**
   GOAL: Understand the problem

3. **Planned Reflection**
   GOAL: Consider possibilities

4. **Action Planning**
   GOAL: Implement the change

Prompted Self-inquiry

Contemplative Writing

Planned Reflection

Action Planning

Step Two: Contemplative Writing

The next stepping-stone of the reflective journaling process is contemplative writing. After you have picked a card, read it, and then write about it. Writing accesses different parts of your brain. It can help you transform obscure, unscripted thoughts and emotions into tangible ideas you can use to reflect on the complex content of your life.

To help you practice this process and integrate what you learn, each journaling page includes three distinct sections: 1) the prewrite activity, 2) the open page with an additional writing prompt, and 3) the reflection activity. Together, they provide a uniform journaling practice that is both thorough and thought-provoking.

Step Three: Planned Reflection

The third stepping-stone of the reflective journaling process is called Planned Reflection. It includes four Planned Reflection pages as well as the Journal Summary section. I purposefully incorporated these five "intentional pauses" into this journal because they are vital components of the Circle of Change.

These breaks from self-discovery offer you an important opportunity to slow down, highlight your strengths, provide positive affirmation, and recognize your growth. Also, besides offering you a chance to nourish your heart, these planned reflection exercises ask you to consider what you really want out of life–including your dreams, intentions, and goals. In the end, this information will help you stay focused.

Step Four: Action Planning

Last but not least, the final stepping-stone of the reflective journaling process is called Action Planning. This stepping-stone is critical to the change process. However, it has consistently proven itself to be the hardest to get through. To ensure you are successful, I have outlined a three things you can to do to avoid getting stuck and/or failing.

1. **Get started**

   Seriously, I'm not kidding. I have watched hundreds of people get stuck before they got started. By default, our species tends to overthink things. Likewise, for many of us, we are perfectionists who set our expectations too high. Just the thought of not achieving what we want can be stifling.

To that point, I am not here to label you or shame you. Nor am I here to tell you to lower your expectations. However, I am here to say, if you want to make a change you need to embrace imperfection, practice and iteration. Shifting gears, learning new things, and working towards balance and fulfillment take time. Plan on being uncomfortable for a bit, not doing it right a couple of times, and adjusting until you are satisfied with the outcome.

2. **Keep going**
Even if *going* means productivity becomes glacial in its progression or you have to take a moment to catch your breath–don't give up. If and when tasks become too large, break them into smaller, more manageable micro-tasks. No one (including yourself) should be pushing you to the finish line before the time is right. The process of change itself will result in greater awareness, wisdom, and conviction. By stretching you will learn about yourself, your circumstances, and the people around you. As a result, you will gain insight into what you value. These are important elements you will need for course modifications and to carry on.

3. **Allow for adjustments**
Slow progress and unexpected challenges can indicate the path you have taken might need adjusting. The success of your journey doesn't depend on how quickly you accomplish your goals. It depends on how accurately they are aligned. Slow down and make sure your efforts are taking you where you want to go. Gift yourself time. It is the healthiest, most sustainable way to grow.

HOW TO USE THE JOURNAL

Because change is complicated and it challenges the best of us, I designed the journaling pages to be pretty easy. Each page includes two sides: the left side and the right side.

The page on the left contains the prewrite and reflection activities while the page on the right is intended to be used for free-writing. At the top of the right page, I have included a daily prompt. These questions ask you to reflect on eight principles I have found useful to the change process. Collectively, I refer to these concepts as the Eight Cardinal Views. They include:

- Self-love
- Personal responsibility
- Self-trust
- Objectivity
- Logic
- Creativity
- Intuition
- Empathy

As you work your way through the journaling pages, you can use the prompts on the open pages to dig deeper into your psyche, values, and beliefs. They were crafted to stretch your soul.

INSTRUCTIONS

When you are ready to start journaling, I have provided specific instructions below outlining how to pull a card and use it with your journal. That being said, what I have offered represents my intentions for the decks and journal. Feel free to customize this reflective journaling experience to meet your needs. This is your chance to own your whole-health and develop the skills and tools you need for your wellness journey.

1. Rest yourself in a quiet space. Firmly plant your feet and position your spine until you feel grounded, well-supported, and connected to the earth. Invite only positive energy to be present. This invitation can be a simple, intuitive agreement with the universe or you can use the divination below:

Let the spirits guide my way,
Share my heart,
Show me light,
Bring me grace,
Hold me tight,
Morning, noon, and night.

ANATOMY OF A CARD

Each card in the three nature-inspired deck series has been arranged in the same manner. For your reference, I have provided a diagram below of the anatomy of each card.*

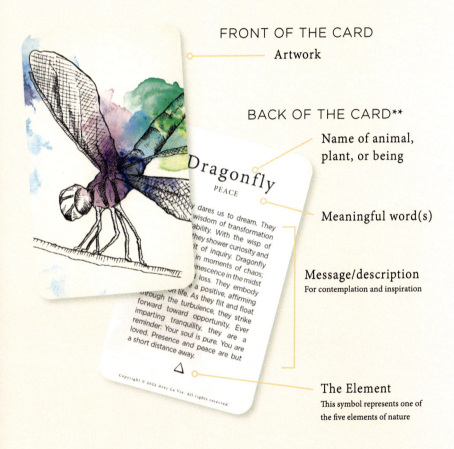

FRONT OF THE CARD
Artwork

BACK OF THE CARD**

Name of animal, plant, or being

Meaningful word(s)

Message/description
For contemplation and inspiration

The Element
This symbol represents one of the five elements of nature

Dragonfly
PEACE

...y dares us to dream. They
...wisdom of transformation
...ability. With the wisp of
...they shower curiosity and
...it of inquiry. Dragonfly
...in moments of chaos;
...inescence in the midst
...l loss. They embody
...e a positive, affirming
...on life. As they flit and float
...through the turbulence, they strike
forward toward opportunity. Ever
imparting tranquility, they are a
reminder: Your soul is pure. You are
loved. Presence and peace are but
a short distance away.

△

---

*I included the copyright information at the bottom of each card because it's common for people to gift individual cards to their family, friends, and colleagues.

**The Flora Healing deck includes the Latin name of the plant underneath the common English name.

BOOST YOUR CARD READINGS

Found items from a simple garden or the land you love
make powerful energetic aids.

MY FAVORITE ENERGETIC AIDS

Various crystals chosen for their unique energies

Garden sage and a self-made wand for purification

Salt for safety and boundary setting

The Element Mandala for universal connection

Candles to represent the element of fire and action

Soil or rocks for grounding

Leaves and feathers to represent clarity

Water to inspire flow and creativity

Plants or flowers to foster growth

2. Take 3 deep breaths in through your mouth and out through your nose.

3. Pick up your deck and shuffle the cards. Once you are ready, select a card. There are no incorrect ways to pull a card. You can take one from the top, the middle, or the back. You could also split the deck and draw a card from the middle. Or, if a card falls out, you can use that card.

4. Before you read your card, fill out the prewrite section. *If you need help identifying your feelings, please reference the Emotion Wheel I have provided on the following pages.*

5. Next, enjoy the art on the front of the card paying particular attention to any thoughts, memories, and/or emotions that present themselves as you examine the art.

6. Then, read the meaningful word and the message on the back of the card. Before moving on, spend a few moments reflecting and paying attention to your thoughts, memories, and/or emotions and exploring what the message means to you.

7. When you are ready, begin writing on the open page to the right. If you would like, incorporate the additional prompt at the top of the page into your journal entry as you process the content from the card.

8. Finish your writing session by closing with the reflection exercise on the lower, left-hand side of the journaling pages.

Every eight pages, complete the Planned Reflection page. Use these four pages as intentional pauses to review and reflect on the previous seven journaling pages.

Once you have used all of the journaling pages and the Planned Reflections, complete the two remaining sections: Journal Summary and Action Planning. These sections are designed to help you consolidate your insights, clarify your soul's intentions, and create action steps to achieve your goals.

You can use this inner inquiry and change management process whenever you feel stuck and/or want to learn more about yourself and the world around you. Reflective journaling is a valuable practice that can foster more balance and joy in your life when used consistently.

IDENTIFYING YOUR EMOTIONS

An integral element of your wellness journey is emotional awareness. It can have a positive effect on how you experience life; particularly your self-esteem and self-confidence. Likewise, it can help you identify how particular situations or individuals might make you feel.

For example, once you know seeing someone might result in feelings of sadness, frustration, or disappointment you can develop a plan for your next encounter. You might set boundaries or practice positive self-talk before you meet. Or, maybe you establish guidelines and expectations. Either way, understanding your emotions is an empowering consequence of self-awareness that can invite intention and balance into your life.

* * *

While you are using this reflective journal, stop and pay attention to how you are feeling. Take note of your emotions before and after each writing session. If you are uncertain about how to name a feeling, you can reference the Emotion Wheel to the right. You can also ask these questions to familiarize yourself with your feelings: What is causing these emotions? What aggravates them? What alleviates them? Are the things I do to address my feelings healthy or harmful to my well-being? What can I do differently?

The more awareness you have of your emotions, the more empathy you can foster for yourself and others during complex situations.

EMOTION WHEEL

*This illustration has been adapted from the Feeling Wheel
created by Dr. Gloria Willcox.*

❋ ❋ ❋

The Emotion Wheel above illustrates your primary and secondary emotions. The large, capitalized words in the center correspond to your six primary emotions: sad, mad, scared, joy, power, and peace. The smaller words within each spoke represent some of the complex secondary emotions you might experience. Use this wheel to "get to know" and understand your emotions. One way to do this is to pay close attention to yourself. When you experience an emotion, consult the wheel and put a name to it. Then, put your emotion into context (i.e., try to understand what you are feeling and why you might be feeling that way).

THE MEANING
OF THE ELEMENTS

A few months before I created my first deck, I had a vision of a mandala. It combined the five elements of nature (e.g., air, water, soil, fire, and essence–or spirit) accompanied by the distinct illustrations used for the art of alchemy. These two pages contain my interpretation of the five elements, The Eight Cardinal Views as well as the symbolism provided by the animals. Combined, they offer additional, synergistic prompts to develop your intuition and foster self-healing with specific emphasis on transformation and growth. If you would like to incorporate these elements into your readings, please visit Exercise 14 in the Advanced Exercises section of the guidebook.

 ESSENCE

Otherwise referred to as ether, Essence represents your spirit / heart and the universal energy that links you to everything else. It is your home and the seat of your soul; the place you return to every day. It is a strong reminder of your interconnectedness with the world around you. Although visibly separate, we are energetically one. Your wellness depends on the health of the whole. This element represents the manifestation of your spirit, your 'why', and the uniqueness of your journey. Connect with Essence for focused intention. Explore this element to nurture the primary Cardinal Views: self-love, self-trust, and personal responsibility.

 AIR

Air represents awakening, reflection, and awareness. It encourages self-exploration, a purposeful approach to understanding your 'soul weight' (the things dragging you down and limiting your flight). Connect with Air to hear what you have been avoiding or denying. Listen intently, breathe in presence and acceptance, and clear energetic congestion to unfold and find your truth. Air encourages you to practice objectivity.

THE MEANING
OF THE ELEMENTS

 WATER

Water represents cleansing. It is also associated with opportunity, possibility, whimsy, flow, and fun. When faced with obstacles (such as internal or external barriers or unexpected turbulence), connect with Water to calm your mind, refresh your spirit, and cultivate courage. Bathe in this element to invite transcendent transformation. Float in fluctuation as you ebb and flow with the tides of change. It represents a wellspring of intuition and creativity.

 SOIL

Soil is grounding to the soul. It is the cornerstone of life, providing the essential ingredients you need for growth: nourishment, stability, and kinship. When you feel depleted or over-run, stop moving and plant yourself. Study the 'soil' around you. Connect with this element when you are ready to do your work, such as: turning things over and/or fertilizing and enriching your surroundings. As hard as it might be, ground yourself in Soil when you need to weed your life, sow new seeds, or harvest a new bounty. This element fosters logic.

 FIRE

Fire symbolizes your heartlight; the energy you need to be productive and manifest your soul's work. It also mirrors your human form's alignment with your authentic truth. When you are out of alignment, Fire will fuel chaos and create darkness. Alternatively, in a state of equilibrium, its energy is a positive catalyst for change. Connect with this element to find where you are imbalanced and then use what you discover to refuel and focus yourself. Fire is the element of empathy.

A JOURNEY OF
inner inquiry

SECTION 2

JOURNALING PAGES

Choosing to be present for your life requires being conscious and purposeful. It means discovering what you value and letting go of the stories that no longer define you. Unpacking those narratives takes work, but with reflection, you can discover their meaning and foster healing. Most importantly, you *can* own your course and manifest a life aligned with your soul's intention.

NAVIGATING
change

I have learned so much about life and death over the past three decades. The bounty of wisdom available to us never ceases to amazing me. As I reflect on how the people I have worked with navigated change in their personal and/or professional life, a few things stand out.

Number one, every one of us will undergo change during our lifetime. Sometimes it is barely perceptible while other times it is explosive, hard, and seemingly insurmountable. Whatever form it takes, change is with us the entirety of our lives.

Second, we are more capable of managing change if we are able to:

- Love ourselves through the process
- Own what we are responsible for
- Trust ourselves to see it through
- And, most importantly, ask others for help when we are struggling

PREWRITE

DATE: _____ DECK: _____

CARD: _____ MEANINGFUL WORD: _____

ELEMENT: _____

BEFORE I BEGIN WRITING:

- What is my intention or question for this moment?
- What am I feeling?

REFLECTION

BEFORE I END WRITING:

- What insight did I gain?
- What am I feeling?
- What would I like to leave on this page?
- What would I like to carry forward with me?

* * *

What does self-love mean to you?

PREWRITE

DATE: _____ DECK:_____

CARD:_____ MEANINGFUL WORD:_____

ELEMENT:_____

BEFORE I BEGIN WRITING:

- What is my intention or question for this moment?
- What am I feeling?

REFLECTION

BEFORE I END WRITING:

- What insight did I gain?
- What am I feeling?
- What would I like to leave on this page?
- What would I like to carry forward with me?

＊　＊　＊

How do you show yourself love?

PREWRITE

DATE: _____ DECK: _____

CARD: _____ MEANINGFUL WORD: _____

ELEMENT: _____

BEFORE I BEGIN WRITING:

- What is my intention or question for this moment?
- What am I feeling?

REFLECTION

BEFORE I END WRITING:

- What insight did I gain?
- What am I feeling?
- What would I like to leave on this page?
- What would I like to carry forward with me?

*　*　*

What things make you feel confident and capable?
(i.e., what are you really good at?)

PREWRITE

DATE: _____   DECK: _____

CARD: _____   MEANINGFUL WORD: _____

ELEMENT: _____

BEFORE I BEGIN WRITING:

- What is my intention or question for this moment?
- What am I feeling?

REFLECTION

BEFORE I END WRITING:

- What insight did I gain?
- What am I feeling?
- What would I like to leave on this page?
- What would I like to carry forward with me?

*   *   *

What things make you feel awkward and uncomfortable?
(i.e., what could use more practice?)

PREWRITE

DATE: _____DECK:_____

CARD:_____MEANINGFUL WORD:_____

ELEMENT:_____

BEFORE I BEGIN WRITING:

- What is my intention or question for this moment?
- What am I feeling?

REFLECTION

BEFORE I END WRITING:

- What insight did I gain?
- What am I feeling?
- What would I like to leave on this page?
- What would I like to carry forward with me?

Who is responsible for fulfilling your dreams?

PREWRITE

DATE: _____ DECK: _____

CARD: _____ MEANINGFUL WORD: _____

ELEMENT: _____

BEFORE I BEGIN WRITING:

- What is my intention or question for this moment?
- What am I feeling?

REFLECTION

BEFORE I END WRITING:

- What insight did I gain?
- What am I feeling?
- What would I like to leave on this page?
- What would I like to carry forward with me?

✳ ✳ ✳

Who keeps you from fulfilling your dreams?

PREWRITE

DATE: _____DECK:_____

CARD:_____MEANINGFUL WORD:_____

ELEMENT:_____

BEFORE I BEGIN WRITING:

- What is my intention or question for this moment?
- What am I feeling?

REFLECTION

BEFORE I END WRITING:

- What insight did I gain?
- What am I feeling?
- What would I like to leave on this page?
- What would I like to carry forward with me?

* * *

What is holding you back or is in your way?

PLANNED
REFLECTION

1. Take a few moments to re-read your last 7 journaling pages. As you reflect on what you have written, consider the following questions.

    - What emotions did I experience over the last 7 days?
    - What emotions, thoughts, or actions did I repeat as I responded to the situations occurring in my life?
    - What positive and/or limiting patterns can I identify?
    - How did I perceive the archetypes or challenges I faced?
    - How did I use what I learned about myself to grow/heal?
    - What did I do to boost my self-confidence?
    - What am I in control of and what can I do to grow/heal?

2. Next, on the following open page, summarize your insights.

3. At the end, set a "soul-stretch" intention and select an action or two you can practice to achieve your goal. In case you are uncertain how to write an intention and subsequent actions, I have provided an example below.

SOUL STRETCH EXAMPLE

Intention: I would like to practice more empathy.

Action: 1) I will acknowledge my biases and 2) listen with objectivity and compassion to improve my understanding of others and their unique situation.

MY SOUL STRETCH

PREWRITE

DATE: _____ DECK: _____

CARD: _____ MEANINGFUL WORD: _____

ELEMENT: _____

BEFORE I BEGIN WRITING:

- What is my intention or question for this moment?
- What am I feeling?

REFLECTION

BEFORE I END WRITING:

- What insight did I gain?
- What am I feeling?
- What would I like to leave on this page?
- What would I like to carry forward with me?

* * *

What would you like to be doing right now?

PREWRITE

DATE: _____ DECK: _____

CARD: _____ MEANINGFUL WORD: _____

ELEMENT: _____

BEFORE I BEGIN WRITING:

- What is my intention or question for this moment?
- What am I feeling?

REFLECTION

BEFORE I END WRITING:

- What insight did I gain?
- What am I feeling?
- What would I like to leave on this page?
- What would I like to carry forward with me?

*   *   *

Where would you like to be in a year?

PREWRITE

DATE: _____ DECK:_____

CARD:_____ MEANINGFUL WORD:_____

ELEMENT:_____

BEFORE I BEGIN WRITING:

- What is my intention or question for this moment?
- What am I feeling?

REFLECTION

BEFORE I END WRITING:

- What insight did I gain?
- What am I feeling?
- What would I like to leave on this page?
- What would I like to carry forward with me?

*　＊　＊*

*Write your life story, the one you would like
to live before you die.*

PREWRITE

DATE: _____ DECK: _____

CARD: _____ MEANINGFUL WORD: _____

ELEMENT: _____

BEFORE I BEGIN WRITING:

- What is my intention or question for this moment?
- What am I feeling?

REFLECTION

BEFORE I END WRITING:

- What insight did I gain?
- What am I feeling?
- What would I like to leave on this page?
- What would I like to carry forward with me?

* * *

Write about a moment from your life that continues to hurt you.
What is painful or hard about that memory?

PREWRITE

DATE: _____ DECK:_____

CARD:_____ MEANINGFUL WORD:_____

ELEMENT:_____

BEFORE I BEGIN WRITING:

- What is my intention or question for this moment?
- What am I feeling?

REFLECTION

BEFORE I END WRITING:

- What insight did I gain?
- What am I feeling?
- What would I like to leave on this page?
- What would I like to carry forward with me?

*   *   *

Write about a moment from your life that lifts you up.
What is inspiring and motivating about that memory?

PREWRITE

DATE: _____ DECK: _____

CARD: _____ MEANINGFUL WORD: _____

ELEMENT: _____

BEFORE I BEGIN WRITING:

- What is my intention or question for this moment?
- What am I feeling?

REFLECTION

BEFORE I END WRITING:

- What insight did I gain?
- What am I feeling?
- What would I like to leave on this page?
- What would I like to carry forward with me?

* * *

Why is objectivity important and how can it be a valuable asset during challenging situations?

PREWRITE

DATE: _____ DECK: _____

CARD: _____ MEANINGFUL WORD: _____

ELEMENT: _____

BEFORE I BEGIN WRITING:

- What is my intention or question for this moment?
- What am I feeling?

REFLECTION

BEFORE I END WRITING:

- What insight did I gain?
- What am I feeling?
- What would I like to leave on this page?
- What would I like to carry forward with me?

*   *   *

*Why is logic important and how can it be a
valuable asset during challenging situations?*

PLANNED REFLECTION

1. Take a few moments to re-read your last 7 journaling pages. As you reflect on what you have written, consider the following questions.

   - What emotions did I experience over the last 7 days?
   - What emotions, thoughts, or actions did I repeat as I responded to the situations occurring in my life?
   - What positive and/or limiting patterns can I identify?
   - How did I perceive the archetypes or challenges I faced?
   - How did I use what I learned about myself to grow/heal?
   - What did I do to boost my self-confidence?
   - What am I in control of and what can I do to grow/heal?

2. Next, on the following open page, summarize your insights.

3. At the end, set a "soul-stretch" intention and select an action or two you can practice to achieve your goal. In case you are uncertain how to write an intention and subsequent actions, I have provided an example below.

SOUL STRETCH EXAMPLE

Intention: I would like to practice more empathy.

Action: 1) I will acknowledge my biases and 2) listen with objectivity and compassion to improve my understanding of others and their unique situation.

MY SOUL STRETCH

PREWRITE

DATE: _____ DECK:_____

CARD:_____ MEANINGFUL WORD:_____

ELEMENT:_____

BEFORE I BEGIN WRITING:

- What is my intention or question for this moment?
- What am I feeling?

REFLECTION

BEFORE I END WRITING:

- What insight did I gain?
- What am I feeling?
- What would I like to leave on this page?
- What would I like to carry forward with me?

* * *

What does personal responsibility mean to you?

PREWRITE

DATE: _____ DECK: _____

CARD: _____ MEANINGFUL WORD: _____

ELEMENT: _____

BEFORE I BEGIN WRITING:

- What is my intention or question for this moment?
- What am I feeling?

REFLECTION

BEFORE I END WRITING:

- What insight did I gain?
- What am I feeling?
- What would I like to leave on this page?
- What would I like to carry forward with me?

Personally and professionally, why is creativity important?

PREWRITE

DATE: _____ DECK: _____

CARD: _____ MEANINGFUL WORD: _____

ELEMENT: _____

BEFORE I BEGIN WRITING:

- What is my intention or question for this moment?
- What am I feeling?

REFLECTION

BEFORE I END WRITING:

- What insight did I gain?
- What am I feeling?
- What would I like to leave on this page?
- What would I like to carry forward with me?

* * *

Who do you know that is creative?
What makes them creative?

PREWRITE

DATE: _____ DECK: _____

CARD: _____ MEANINGFUL WORD: _____

ELEMENT: _____

BEFORE I BEGIN WRITING:

- What is my intention or question for this moment?
- What am I feeling?

REFLECTION

BEFORE I END WRITING:

- What insight did I gain?
- What am I feeling?
- What would I like to leave on this page?
- What would I like to carry forward with me?

* * *

List at least five ways you are creative.

PREWRITE

DATE: _____DECK:_____

CARD:_____MEANINGFUL WORD:_____

ELEMENT:_____

BEFORE I BEGIN WRITING:

- What is my intention or question for this moment?
- What am I feeling?

REFLECTION

BEFORE I END WRITING:

- What insight did I gain?
- What am I feeling?
- What would I like to leave on this page?
- What would I like to carry forward with me?

*　*　*

How can self-expression help you achieve your life goals?

PREWRITE

DATE: _____ DECK:_____

CARD:_____ MEANINGFUL WORD:_____

ELEMENT:_____

BEFORE I BEGIN WRITING:

- What is my intention or question for this moment?
- What am I feeling?

REFLECTION

BEFORE I END WRITING:

- What insight did I gain?
- What am I feeling?
- What would I like to leave on this page?
- What would I like to carry forward with me?

*   *   *

What does self-trust mean to you?

PREWRITE

DATE: _____ DECK:_____

CARD:_____ MEANINGFUL WORD:_____

ELEMENT:_____

BEFORE I BEGIN WRITING:

- What is my intention or question for this moment?
- What am I feeling?

REFLECTION

BEFORE I END WRITING:

- What insight did I gain?
- What am I feeling?
- What would I like to leave on this page?
- What would I like to carry forward with me?

*   *   *

How can self-trust help you achieve your life goals?

PLANNED REFLECTION

1. Take a few moments to re-read your last 7 journaling pages. As you reflect on what you have written, consider the following questions.

   - What emotions did I experience over the last 7 days?
   - What emotions, thoughts, or actions did I repeat as I responded to the situations occurring in my life?
   - What positive and/or limiting patterns can I identify?
   - How did I perceive the archetypes or challenges I faced?
   - How did I use what I learned about myself to grow/heal?
   - What did I do to boost my self-confidence?
   - What am I in control of and what can I do to grow/heal?

2. Next, on the following open page, summarize your insights.

3. At the end, set a "soul-stretch" intention and select an action or two you can practice to achieve your goal. In case you are uncertain how to write an intention and subsequent actions, I have provided an example below.

SOUL STRETCH EXAMPLE

Intention: I would like to practice more empathy.

Action: 1) I will acknowledge my biases and 2) listen with objectivity and compassion to improve my understanding of others and their unique situation.

MY SOUL STRETCH

PREWRITE

DATE: _____ DECK: _____

CARD: _____ MEANINGFUL WORD: _____

ELEMENT: _____

BEFORE I BEGIN WRITING:

- What is my intention or question for this moment?
- What am I feeling?

REFLECTION

BEFORE I END WRITING:

- What insight did I gain?
- What am I feeling?
- What would I like to leave on this page?
- What would I like to carry forward with me?

* * *

*Describe intuition and how it can help
you achieve your life goals.*

PREWRITE

DATE: _____ DECK: _____

CARD: _____ MEANINGFUL WORD: _____

ELEMENT: _____

BEFORE I BEGIN WRITING:

- What is my intention or question for this moment?
- What am I feeling?

REFLECTION

BEFORE I END WRITING:

- What insight did I gain?
- What am I feeling?
- What would I like to leave on this page?
- What would I like to carry forward with me?

* * *

Are you satisfied with your personal life? Explain.

PREWRITE

DATE: _____ DECK: _____

CARD: _____ MEANINGFUL WORD: _____

ELEMENT: _____

BEFORE I BEGIN WRITING:
- What is my intention or question for this moment?
- What am I feeling?

REFLECTION

BEFORE I END WRITING:
- What insight did I gain?
- What am I feeling?
- What would I like to leave on this page?
- What would I like to carry forward with me?

*   *   *

*If you could change two things about your personal life,
what would they be?*

PREWRITE

DATE: _____ DECK:_____

CARD:_____ MEANINGFUL WORD:_____

ELEMENT:_____

BEFORE I BEGIN WRITING:

- What is my intention or question for this moment?
- What am I feeling?

REFLECTION

BEFORE I END WRITING:

- What insight did I gain?
- What am I feeling?
- What would I like to leave on this page?
- What would I like to carry forward with me?

* * *

Are you satisfied with your professional life? Explain.

PREWRITE

DATE: _____ DECK:_____

CARD:_____ MEANINGFUL WORD:_____

ELEMENT:_____

BEFORE I BEGIN WRITING:

- What is my intention or question for this moment?
- What am I feeling?

REFLECTION

BEFORE I END WRITING:

- What insight did I gain?
- What am I feeling?
- What would I like to leave on this page?
- What would I like to carry forward with me?

*If you could change two things about your professional life,
what would they be?*

PREWRITE

DATE: _____DECK:_____

CARD:_____MEANINGFUL WORD:_____

ELEMENT:_____

BEFORE I BEGIN WRITING:

- What is my intention or question for this moment?
- What am I feeling?

REFLECTION

BEFORE I END WRITING:

- What insight did I gain?
- What am I feeling?
- What would I like to leave on this page?
- What would I like to carry forward with me?

*   *   *

Who in your life is important to you?
How do they help you or limit you from achieving your life goals?

PREWRITE

DATE: _____ DECK: _____

CARD: _____ MEANINGFUL WORD: _____

ELEMENT: _____

BEFORE I BEGIN WRITING:

- What is my intention or question for this moment?
- What am I feeling?

REFLECTION

BEFORE I END WRITING:

- What insight did I gain?
- What am I feeling?
- What would I like to leave on this page?
- What would I like to carry forward with me?

*   *   *

Who in your life challenges you?
How do they help you or limit you from achieving your life goals?

PLANNED REFLECTION

1. Take a few moments to re-read your last 7 journaling pages. As you reflect on what you have written, consider the following questions.

   - What emotions did I experience over the last 7 days?
   - What emotions, thoughts, or actions did I repeat as I responded to the situations occurring in my life?
   - What positive and/or limiting patterns can I identify?
   - How did I perceive the archetypes or challenges I faced?
   - How did I use what I learned about myself to grow/heal?
   - What did I do to boost my self-confidence?
   - What am I in control of and what can I do to grow/heal?

2. Next, on the following open page, summarize your insights.

3. At the end, set a "soul-stretch" intention and select an action or two you can practice to achieve your goal. In case you are uncertain how to write an intention and subsequent actions, I have provided an example below.

SOUL STRETCH EXAMPLE

Intention: I would like to practice more empathy.

Action: 1) I will acknowledge my biases and 2) listen with objectivity and compassion to improve my understanding of others and their unique situation.

* * *

If you were your own best friend,
what would you tell yourself right now?

MY SOUL STRETCH

REFLECTION
for growth

SECTION 3

JOURNAL SUMMARY

Implicit to the idea of living a conscious, purposeful life
is making the choice to enjoy your existence.

YOUR WELLNESS BEGINS WITH YOU

Those old adages, *be the change you wish to see* and *change begins with you*, are actually true. Once you become an adult and you are able to manage your own affairs, your well-being is your responsibility. No one can or will ever know you as well as you.

Swan
LOVE

Swan teaches about the power of self-love. Drawing upon the energy of our virtue, they encourage us to reflect upon our fortuitous bounty as humans. In the embrace of their grace, we are reminded to gently swim with the current rather than aggressively against it. When you are faced with strong emotions, receive and validate them with empathy. Like you, they deserve to be acknowledged. Once they are, healing can occur. Shame is not necessary in those moments. Offer yourself compassion. Show yourself some love.

Likewise, no one can prescribe or tell you how to achieve balance, fulfillment, or joy. Only you can decide for yourself who you are, what you value, and how you will experience this lifetime.

When I have witnessed individuals, families, and teams believe in themselves, literally anything was possible. Why? Because everything they did was grounded in self-awareness and self-trust. They pushed past delay and self-doubt. They showed-up for themselves, the people in their life, and every endeavor they undertook. In the end, they shared everything unique and beautiful about who they were without embarrassment, excuses, or shame.

Now, with 28-days of inner inquiry behind you, it is time for you to show-up for yourself. It's time to look forward, fall in love with everything you are, and manifest your heart's desires.

Growth Channeling

Congratulations my friend! Over the past few weeks you have
spent a lot of time reflecting on who you are and the world you live in.
Now it is time to hone in on your soul's intentions.

A-HA No. 1

What did you learn about yourself?
strengths & weaknesses

A-HA No. 2

What are your life goals?

soul intentions

A-HA No. 3

What things ignite you?
awaken & excite your spirit

A-HA No. 4

What things challenge you?
good ways & hard ways

A-HA No. 5

What things do you want to change?
*self * family * work * community*

A-HA No. 6

What things do you want to keep the same?

self * *family* * *work* * *community*

TURNING
ideas into action

SECTION 4

ACTION PLANNING

HORTICULTURE
PERSONIFIED

Before we get started on this section, I would like to share a short story with you. I am a perennial gardener and my neighbor is a heirloom vegetable gardener. Our yards are vastly different but they are equally beautiful.

Since I love flowers, I have spent years moving rock, amending soil, and planting perennials that bring visual joy year after year. He has done the same but with a different intention. He wanted to create a regenerative suburban yard and harvest organic, wholesome food that would nourish his family.

This conscious, purposeful work we undertook, I call: Horticulture Personified. Although it hearkens to gardening, this phrase means so much more. It represents the embodiment of our efforts to cultivate the bounty we wish to realize. While our outcomes might be different, my neighbor and I had to identify what we wanted, plan how we would achieve it, and take action to make it happen. Now, years later, we are enjoying our amazing gardens.

Welcome to the magical world of manifestation. It's time to turn your ideas into reality and reap the benefits of all your hard work.

WELCOME TO THE
magical world of manifestation

Picture this...

Do you wish your life looked a particular way?
Well then, illustrate what you want to see.
Use these pages to draw and make notes about how you
want to live and what you want to see in your life.

Your Manifestation Plan

Now that you have envisioned what you want,
it is time to turn your ideas into reality!

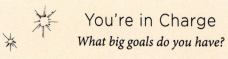

You're in Charge
What big goals do you have?

GOAL 1

☐ Personal Goal   ☐ Professional Goal

GOAL 2

☐ Personal Goal   ☐ Professional Goal

GOAL 3

☐ Personal Goal   ☐ Professional Goal

GOAL 4

☐ Personal Goal   ☐ Professional Goal

How will you make your goals happen?

For each goal, create a list of action steps to manifest your ideas

GOAL 1
action steps

To accomplish this goal, I will need to:

When do I want to achieve this goal?

What help will I need?

GOAL 2
action steps

To accomplish this goal, I will need to:

When do I want to achieve this goal?

What help will I need?

GOAL 3
action steps

To accomplish this goal, I will need to:

When do I want to achieve this goal?

What help will I need?

GOAL 4
action steps

To accomplish this goal, I will need to:

When do I want to achieve this goal?

What help will I need?

Timing is Key

Hooray! You're on your way.
Take a few moments to prioritize and organize your energy.
Use the next few pages to plan your success...
and then get going!

GOAL 1

Action Steps	Complete By
1	
2	
3	
4	
5	
6	
7	
8	
9	
10	

*   *   *

Remember to believe in yourself!

you can do this

GOAL 2

Action Steps	Complete By
1	
2	
3	
4	
5	
6	
7	
8	
9	
10	

GOAL 3

Action Steps	Complete By
1	
2	
3	
4	
5	
6	
7	
8	
9	
10	

✳ ✳ ✳

While you're at it, have some fun!

GOAL 4

Action Steps	Complete By
1	
2	
3	
4	
5	
6	
7	
8	
9	
10	

Self-care Routine

Change is hard, but it is easy to loose yourself in it.
Make a list of ways to nurture yourself while you're
manifesting your intentions and dreams.

P.S. DON'T FORGET TO
HOWL AT THE MOON
lighten up, it's fun!

REFERENCES

Abbott, P., & Meerabeau, L. (Eds.). (1998). *The sociology of the caring professions* (2nd ed.). Philadelphia, PA: UCL Press.

Aguilar, E. (2013). *The art of coaching: Effective strategies for school transformation*. San Francisco, CA: John Wiley & Sons, Inc.

Anderson, D.L. (2012). *Organization development: The process of leading organizational change*. Thousand Oaks, CA: Sage Publications, Inc.

Burack-Weiss, Q., Lawrence, L. S., & Bamat Mijangos, L. (Eds.). (2017). *Narrative in social work practice: The power and possibility of story*. New York, NY: Columbia University Press.

Centers for Disease Control and Prevention. *Facts about suicide*. Retrieved from: https://www.cdc.gov/suicide/facts/index.html

Consilio, Jennifer, & Kennedy, Sheila M. (2019). Using mindfulness as a heuristic for writing evaluation: Transforming pedagogy and quality of experience. [Special issue on contemplative writing across the disciplines.] Across the Disciplines, 16(1), 28-49. Retrieved from http://wac.colostate.edu/docs/atd/contemplative/consilio_kennedy2019.pdf

Cottle, T. J. (2003). *A sense of self: The work of affirmation*. Boston, MA: University of Massachusetts Press.

Eurich, T. (2018). *What self-awareness really is (and how to cultivate it)*. Harvard Business Review. Retrieved from https://hbr.org/2018/01/what-self-awareness-really-is-and-how-to-cultivate-it

Freud, S. (1913). *The interpretation of dreams*. New York, NY: The MacMillan Company.

Greater Good in Education. *Contemplative Writing*. Retrieved from https://ggie.berkeley.edu/practice/contemplative-writing/

Hobson, J. A. (1999). *Dreaming as delirium: How the brain goes out of its mind*. Cambridge, MA: A Bradford Book. The MIT Press.

Holman, P., Devane, T., & Cady, S. (Eds.). (2007). *The change handbook: The definitive resource on today's best methods for engaging whole systems*. San Francisco, CA: Berret-Koehler Publishers, Inc.

Kinane, K. (2019). The place of practice in contemplative pedagogy and writing. [Special issue on contemplative writing across the disciplines.] Across the Disciplines, 16(1), 6-15. Retrieved from http://wac.colostate.edu/docs/atd/contemplative/kinane2019.pdf

Kinane, K. (2019) Critical, creative, contemplative. Contemplative pedagogy and the religious studies classroom: Spotlight on teaching, June, 21-25. Retrieved from https://rsn.aarweb.org/spotlight-on/teaching/contemplative-pedagogy/criticalcreativecontemplative

Mayo Clinic. Suicide and suicidal thoughts. Retrieved from https://www.mayoclinic.org/diseases-conditions/suicide/symptoms-causes/syc-20378048#:~:text=Experience%20a%20stressful%20life%20event,to%20act%20on%20your%20thoughts

McLean, G. N. (2006). *Organization development: Principles, processes, performance*. Oakland, CA: Berrett-Koehler Publishers, Inc.

McTighe, J. P. (2018). *Narrative theory in clinical social work practice*. Middletown, DE: Springer Nature.

Miller, Marlowe, & Kinane, Karolyn. (2019). Contemplative writing across the disciplines. [Special issue on contemplative writing across the disciplines.] Across the Disciplines, 16(1), 1-5. Retrieved from http://wac.colostate.edu/docs/atd/contemplative/intro.pdf

Murphy-Hiscock, A. (2017). *The green witch: Your complete guide to the natural magic of herbs, flowers, essential oils, and more*. Avon: MA: Simon and Schuster, Inc.

Murphy-Hiscock, A. (2020). *The green witch's Grimoire: Your complete guide to creating your own book of natural magic*. Avon: MA: Simon and Schuster, Inc.

Narrative Therapy Centre. *About narrative therapy*. Retrieved from https://narrativetherapycentre.com/about/

National Center for Biotechnology Information. The origin and evolution of cells. Retrieved from https://www.ncbi.nlm.nih.gov/books/NBK9841/#:~:text=Present%2Dday%20cells%20evolved%20from,aerobic%20(more...)

National Geographic. *How many species haven't we found yet?* Retrieved from https://www.nationalgeographic.com/newsletters/animals/article/how-many-species-have-not-found-december-26

New York Times. Meet LUCA, the ancestor of all living things. Retrieved from https://www.nytimes.com/2016/07/26/science/last-universal-ancestor.html

Patterson, K., Grenny, J., McMillan, R., & Switzler, A. (2012). *Crucial conversations: Tools for talking when stakes are high* (2nd ed.). New York: NY: McGraw-Hill Books.

Rosen, R. *Intuition 101: Developing your clairsenses*. Retrieved from https://www.oprah.com/spirit/developing-your-5-clair-senses-rebecca-rosen/all

Rothwell, W. J., Stavros, J. M., & Sullivan, R. L. (Eds.) (2016). *Practicing organization development: Leading transformation and change (4th ed.)*. Hoboken, NJ: John Wiley & Sons, Inc.

Shetty, J. (2020). *Think like a monk: Train your mind for peace and purpose every day*. New York, NY: Simon & Schuster

University of Minnesota. *Introductory biology: Evolutionary and ecological perspectives, chapter 87. The plant kingdom*. Retrieved from https://pressbooks.umn.edu/introbio/chapter/plantskingdom/

Walker, J., Payne, S., Jarrett, N., & Ley, T. (Eds.). *Psychology for nurses and the caring professions (4th ed.)*. New York, NY: Open University Press.

Western Connecticut State University. *What is holistic health?* Retrieved from https://www.wcsu.edu/ihhs/what-is-holistic-health/#:~:text=Holistic%20health%20is%20an%20approach,social%2C%20intellectual%2C%20and%20spiritual.

World Health Organization. *Suicide*. Retrieved from https://www.who.int/news-room/fact-sheets/detail/suicide

MORNING, NOON *&* NIGHT

Let the spirits guide my way,
Share my heart,
Show me light,
Bring me grace,
Hold me tight,
Morning, noon, and night.

– Rebecca Lefebvre